Buy, Hold, and Sell

Automated trading for every income

By: Shanelle Woodard

Copyright 2016

Woodard Holdings, LLC

ISBN-13: 978-1534715431

ISBN-10: 1534715436

BISAC: Business & Economics/ Investments & Securities/ Stocks

Dedication

To my father, who through conversation of enlightenment birthed this book!

-Thank you

In loving memory of

Marvin Darden

Christine Darden-Trotter

Content

Introduction

Introduction

Everyone says that they can't put away $5.00 to save. Or they don't know how to invest their money, or they don't understand trading. But what if I told you in this little book I will give you all the fundamental tools you need to make stock trades to start building an infrastructure of income and financial growth. In this book I teach you how to automat your stock trades so you can use time wisely and be able to make money while you are involved in other endeavors.

In this book we will dig into what stocks are, how they work for you, and what rights you have as a shareholder in a company. This book will also explain how to use as little as $40 a month to build a portfolio that may grow quicker than your 401k that you put the equivalent amount in, because of the lessor amount of fees you will be paying plus the compounding that you will be receiving from each of your trades. See most 401k's invest into ETF's or what we call exchange traded funds which give you smaller returns, instead of investing in dividend producing stocks.

I believe that we can all succeed in this race of wealth by realizing that now thanks to the internet we are no longer priced out of the Wall Street game. We just have to learn the game in the way that it facilitates to us as a whole.

Chapter 1

The Stock market and the internet

Chapter 1

The Stock market and the internet

The stock market as we knew it in the past has changed. No need to call up a broker, and spend hundreds of dollars all at once to make a trade. Or even worry about having that pesky $500-$5,000 minimum to trade. A lot of us felt we were priced out of the stock market. Now that the internet has come and taken over the investment market you don't have to worry about being a millionaire to make a trade you just have to be smart in your trading. You can take as little as $5 and tuck it away in a stock. The little man is not priced out of the stock market now. All you need is time, dividends, capital gains, and a game plan and you are good to go.

Now we have T.D. Ameritrade, E-trader, Capital one investing, Robin Hood, and etc. as a platform to make our trades on. We don't have to go through the traditional broker over the phone or walk in a brokerage firm on wall street we can do it ourselves with lower fees and hassle. The wider availability of information because of what we have nickname Google University or google as we naturally call it has opened up new doors for us individuals who have been interested in stocks. We no longer have to go to the library to learn about how to trade stocks and to look up company information we can do it from the comfort of our own homes now.

With the Internet we can go online to the SEC (Securities and Exchange Commission) website and look up company reports. Just search and download a company statement in lightning speeds.

Let's not forget how cheap commission rates have become now with online brokerage firms. So with all these positives the internet has placed the power all in your hands to invest your money and to make great financial decisions for your investments.

In this book we will be using discount brokers to trade with. Let me explain what a discount broker is, a discount broker is a stock broker who executes our buy and sell orders at a low commission fee. However they do not offer investment advice to individuals who use their services. However, that's ok because I will teach you in this book the fundamentals that you will need to handle that part yourself. So without further a due let's jump into it with chapter 2.

Chapter 2

The fundamentals to investing

Chapter 2

The fundamentals to investing

Now let's start out by breaking down the fundamental terms that you will need to know and understand in order to invest. I also explain in this chapter how to understand a stock summary page and chart. Now the stock market opens at 9:30 a.m. and closes at 4 p.m., however after hour quotes run for 3 hours after the stock market closes. So if you ever go to look at a stock price hours after the market closes and it's different from the amount you seen at 4 p.m. don't panic it's just the system trying to process the last remaining trades that went through before 4p.m.

Stocks:

So what is a stock? A stock is an asset that appreciates or depreciates over time. A stock signifies ownership in a corporation and gives you claim on part of the corporation's assets and earnings. There are two main types of stocks which are:

Two main types of stocks:

Common stock:

> Common stock is an ownership in a publicly traded corporation, which usually allows the owner of the shares to vote at shareholder's meetings and to receive dividends.

It gives the holder four distinct rights:

1. able to transfer ownership of stock shares by sales or gift to someone.

2. able to inspect company's books, records, minutes from shareholder meetings.

3. able to vote on company's important affairs.

4. Maintain a proportionate share of ownership by purchasing a proportionate share of any new stock issued.

Preferred stock:

Preferred stock holders don't have voting rights, but has a higher claim on assets and earnings then the common shareholders, and they also typically get paid a steady dividend.

Ex. owners of preferred stock receive dividends before common shareholders and have priority in the event that a company goes bankrupt and is liquidated.

Shareholder:

What is a shareholder? It's any person, company that owns at least one share of a company's stock. Shareholders are a company's owners. Shareholders have the opportunity to profit if a company does well or the potential to lose if the company performs poorly.

Shareholders are also referred to as a "stockholder".

Shareholder rights:

Shareholders rights are defined in a corporation's charter and bylaws. You have the right to inspect the company's books and records, sue the corporation for misdeeds of the directors and officers, and if the company happens to liquidate, they have a right to a share of the proceeds. However preferred stock holders have precedence over common stock holders in liquidation. Shareholders also have the rights to receive a portion of any dividends the company declares. Shareholders have the right to attend the corporation's annual meetings to learn about the company's performance.

Now that we understand what a stock is and what rights we have once we invest in them, let's look at the most talked about stock exchanges and get an idea of what they are. A stock exchange is where stocks are sold and bought. The following is a list of the top 3 stock exchanges.

List of top 3 stock exchanges:

- NYSE- (New York stock exchange) is the world's largest stock exchange by market capitalization.

- NASDAQ- This is the second largest exchange in the world based on its market capitalization. It holds some of the world's largest technology companies, such as Apple.

- OTC market Group- (over the counter securities) these are very risky investments with very small market capitalization. When people bring up penny stocks the majority of the time they purchase them from this exchange.

Let me take a minute before we go any further and explain what market capitalization is. Market capitalization is the market value of a company's outstanding shares. For example if Woodard holdings was trading on the stock market at $10 per share and had a million shares outstanding then the company market capitalization would be $10 million. This would make the stock a micro-cap stock. So let's go over the 5 basic stock categories of market capitalization.

5 basic stock categories of market capitalization:

- Micro Cap (under $250 million) the smallest stocks on the stock market and the riskiest available. Micro Cap stocks would be penny stocks, which are stocks that sell for $10 or less.

- Small Cap ($250 million to $2 billion) these stocks have little growth potential. There is a moderate amount of risk with these stocks.

- Mid Cap ($2 billion to $5 billion) these stocks have safety and growth potential.

- Large Cap ($5 billion to $25 billion) good for conservative stock investors who want steady appreciation with greater safety, these stocks are also called blue chip stocks. The Dow Jones Industrial Average carries a lot of these stocks. These are very low risk stocks, for example Walt Disney or Microsoft would be good to use as a reference for a large cap stock.

- Ultra Cap (over $25 billion) mega caps, companies that are the biggest on the market. Stocks such as general electric and Exxon Mobil would be considered Ultra Cap stocks.

In this next section we will talk about what a ticker symbol is, Securities transactions (filling and confirming orders), and the two ways to buy securities, and the different stock buy / sell orders.

Ticker Symbol:

A ticker symbol is an abbreviation used to uniquely identify publicly traded shares of a stock on a particular stock market. It may consist of letters, numbers or a combination of both.

Ex. fb which is the ticker symbol for Facebook.

So here it is first you have to find the ticker symbol of the company you want to invest in. You can find ticker symbols by putting in the company's name in Google's search engine and finding the ticker symbol that way, or by using Nasdaq.com, or actual brokerage websites.

Securities transactions- filling and confirming orders:

When making a stock trade order tickets must contain the following:

1. Buy or sell

2. If a sell, "short" or "long"

3. Account number

4. Type of account

5. Security's ticker symbol

6. Quantity of shares

7. Type of order

8. Account executive ID number

9. Discretion qualifiers, if any

Two ways to buy securities:

Primary market- securities are issued directly by the corporation or agency seeking to raise funds.

Secondary market- securities that are being bought and sold by investors.

Different stock buy/ sell orders are:

- **Market order**- Is the default, it is the order to buy or sell securities at the current market price.

- **Limit order**- is an order to buy or sell securities at a particular price. The broker executing the order may use their discretion to buy or sell at a set amount beyond the limit if they feel it is necessary to fill the order.

- **Stop-loss order**- is an order placed to buy or sell once a stock reaches a specific price. It's design to limit an investor's loss on a security. For example, setting a stop-loss-order for 5% below the price at which you bought the stock will limit your loss to 5%.

- **Day order**- expires at the end of the trading day.

Now we are going to learn about stock summaries and tables. It's absolutely important that we understand clearly the story that the stock summary is trying to explain to use. And when I say **story** I mean what the numbers are trying to tell us about the past and present situation of a company. So let's examine understanding stock summaries and table's number 1.

Understanding Stock summaries and tables example 1:

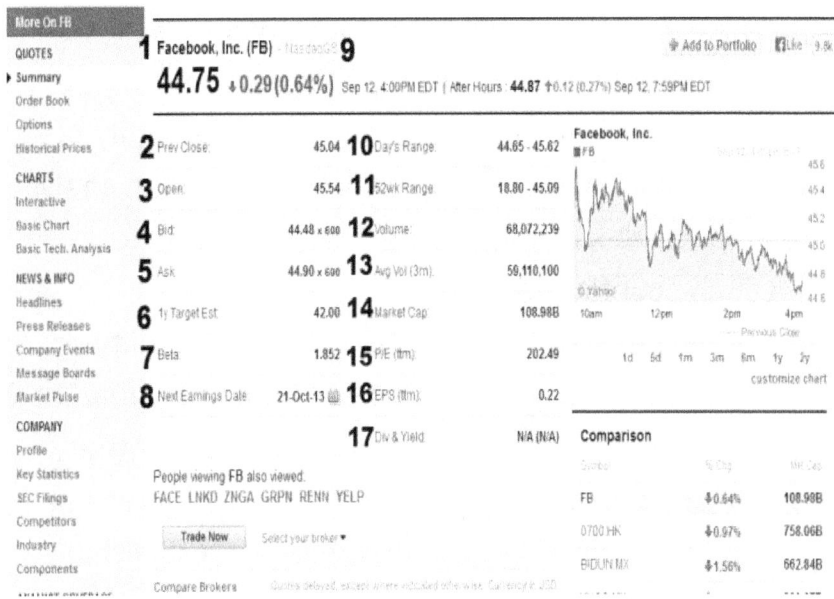

1. Name and symbol- The name of the company of the stock and the stock symbol that is used to identify the stock on the stock exchange.
2. Prev Close- The amount the stock price

closed at on the previous trading day.

3. Open- How much the stock price was at the open of the stock market on the current trading day.

4. Bid- Is the buy price of the stock.

5. Ask- Is the selling price of the stock.

6. 1y target estimate- is what analyst considered the stock price will be one year from now. If this number is higher than the current stock price analyst think highly of the stock. If this number is low, then analyst think poorly of this stock and have no confidence in it.

7. Beta- is a measure of a stocks volatility or level of risk, compared to the stock market as a whole. A Beta of 1 is a sign that the stock will move with the stock market as a whole. A Beta of less than 1 is a sign that the stock will be less volatile than the stock market. A stock with a Beta of more than one indicates that the stock will be more volatile than the stock market, which means bigger risk but a possibility of a greater rate of return.

8. Next earnings date- The date of the

company's next release of the company's earnings report.

9. NASDAQ- the stock exchange that this particular stock is being traded on. The exchange will always be by the name of the company and ticker symbol on a stock summary.

10. Day's Range- The price range of the stock on that specific trading day.

11. 52 week range- The range of the stock lowest to highest price in the last 52 weeks of trading.

12. Volume- The amount of shares that have been traded during a given trading day.

13. Average volume- the total amount of shares traded in a period, divided by the length of time. (For our example the length of time is 3 months.)

14. Market Cap- (Market Capitalization) the market value of a company's outstanding shares. We use the following formula to come up with this number:
    Stock price x total number of shares Outstanding

15. P/E- (price-to-earnings ratio) a valuation

ratio of the company's current share price compared to its per-share earnings. You want to buy stocks with a low P/E ratio. Also compare the stocks that you are interested in P/E ratio to other companies in the same sector.

16. EPS- (Earnings per share) is the monetary of earning per outstanding share of common stock for a company.

17. Div & Yield- (dividend and yield) the dividend is the amount of money paid to an investor from the company's profits either quarterly or annually. The yield is the dividend express as a percentage.

The next chart gives another example of the stock summary and table. It's just set up in a different way. As you go on your journey of researching stocks you will notice that not every research site has all the same information or have their stock summary set up the same. In Understanding Stock summaries and tables example 2, I will explain the different terminology used and point out the similarities.

Understanding Stock summaries and tables

example 2

Starbucks Corporation (SBUX) - NASDAQ

$51.13 ↓ -0.40 (-0.77%)

10:33 AM, 06/09 - BATS BZX Real-Time Price

52wk high:	52.46
52wk low:	35.38
EPS:	1.70
PE (ttm):	30.40
Div Rate:	0.64
Yield:	1.24
Market Cap:	$77.32b
Volume:	1,107,563

5 Day Price - SBUX

June 9, 2015 © quotemedia.com

Today **5d** 1m 3m 1y 5y 10y

39,821 people get SBUX breaking news and analysis by email alert.

Get email alerts on SBUX »

52 week high- Is the highest amount the stock traded for in the last 52 weeks.

52 week low- Is the lowest the stock traded for in the last 52 weeks.

EPS and P/E we have gone over with the previous example. Refer back to Understanding Stock summaries and tables example 1.

Div Rate- The total amount of dividend payments a year.

Yield, Market Cap, and Volume we have gone over in the example chart; Understanding Stock summaries and tables example 1, refer back to that.

Now that you have a better understanding of the chart summary and the terminology used we now will look at how to make a stock trade.

Chapter 3

How to plan out your portfolio

Chapter 3

How to plan out your portfolio

Alright, the number one investment rule is to never invest all your money in one stock. Spread your money out between different investments. Make sure you check your portfolio at least every other month to make sure no drastic changes or losses have occurred. You want to commit your investments for 5 years or longer.

A stock portfolio is a group of assets such as exchange traded funds, stocks, bonds, and cash. Well-built stock portfolios can outperform other investments over time.

Now to build your portfolio you first have to ask yourself a set of questions:

1. How old are you?
2. How old would you like to be at retirement?
3. How much risk can you tolerate?
4. What is your overall goal amount?
5. How much are you willing to invest?
6. How much time are you willing to let your

investment grow?

7. Are you investing for income?

Now that you have answered those seven questions let's look at your portfolio risk factor. Now say you are young, maybe 30 years old or younger you can do more risky investments than say a person 31 or older, because you have more time on your hands to let your investments grown and rebuild from losses. The older you are the least amount of risk you want to take and you want to focus more investing into income producing stock, because that will one day substitute your current income.

Example of Investment strategy:

If you set aside $40 a month to invest you would:

1. Automate your investment account to take $10 out of your checking account every week.
2. Automate your investment to make one monthly trade a month once your account balance totals $40.

3. Pick what stocks you would like to invest in and establish it into your automated plan and set how much each stock will get out of the $40 a month. (I would suggest you only trade one or two stocks if you will only have a monthly investment of $40).
4. Automate your account to reinvest all dividends paid out into the stock that paid it. (That will keep you from having to pay more fees if you wanted to use the dividends to buy more stocks).
5. You can stop the automated process at any time or decrease or increase to the amount of cash you would like to trade with.

It is very important that you diversify you portfolio holdings across different sectors to lower your overall risk. (A sector is a category a stock is placed into, for example financial, utilities, transportation.)

Chapter 4

How to do the research

Chapter 4

How to do the research

Doing the research is a little more strenuous. It takes some time and effort, but if it is done right the return is well worth it.

When doing your stock research you must examine company's competitors. How are they comparing to their business performance? Are they generating more revenue? What is the market capitalization of the other competitors in the same sector compared to yours?

You must research several stocks in one sector or industry so you can compare market performance. Also check the company's earnings forecast.

Analyze a company's financial statements and all other available information about the company. The financial statements you should look at are the balance sheet, income statement, and cash flow statement. Let me explain to you what these financial statements actually contain and why they matter so much in your research.

Balance sheet:

The balance sheet is a financial statement that tells a company's assets, liabilities, and shareholders' equity at a particular point and time. These three sheets that make up the balance sheet give you an idea as to what the company owns and owes, and the amount that shareholders have invested into the company. What you are looking for is a balance sheet is at least 5 years of asset growth and a decline in liabilities. The formula we use to determine the numeric example of these sheets is:

Assets=Liabilities + shareholder's equity

Income statement:

An income statement measures a company's performance over a specific accounting period. This statement gives a picture of how the company incurs its revenue and expenses through operating and non-operating activities. It also show the net profit or loss the company incurred over a specific accounting period, typically a fiscal quarter or year.

Cash flow statement:

Cash flow statement is a quarterly report that must be disclosed to the SEC and the public by every publicly traded company. This document provides information on all cash inflows a company receives from its ongoing operations and external investment sources, as well as all cash outflows that pay for business activities and investments during a quarter.

Long story short, you want each one of these statements to show profit growth every year. You also want these statements to show a drop in liabilities every year and to also show a payout from profits in dividends. Below is a list of websites you can use to do your research with. Please make sure you do your due diligence before investing.

Research Websites to use:

CNN money.com

nasdaq.com

bloomberg.com

Yahoo finance.com

MSN.com

Google finance.com

Morning star.com

When looking at the chart patterns you want to look at stocks with an upward trend. The upward trend must be consistent for at least 10 years or more. Since we are trading automated you will incur less risk with a stock with steady growth.

You must look at the dividend payouts to see if:

1. If the company pays out a dividend. The below chart shows a company that pays out its dividend consistently.

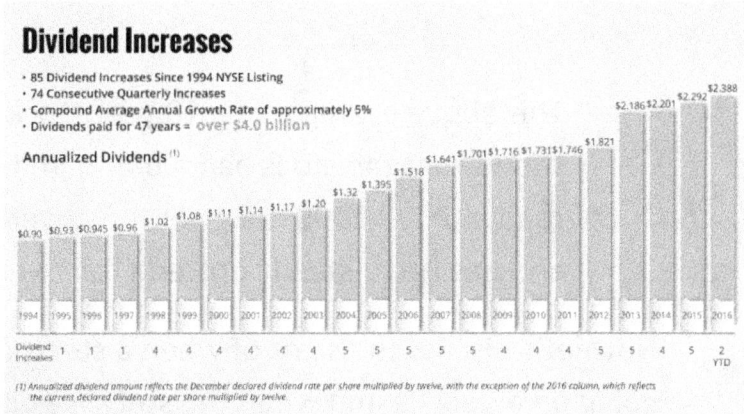

2. If the payouts have grown in the last 7 to 10 years consistently. The previous chart shows an example of a company that has had dividend growth for over 7 years.
3. If the company revenue has grown for at least five years.
4. If the company annual dividend percentage is more than 3%
5. If the stock has a steady 10 to 20 year uptrend.

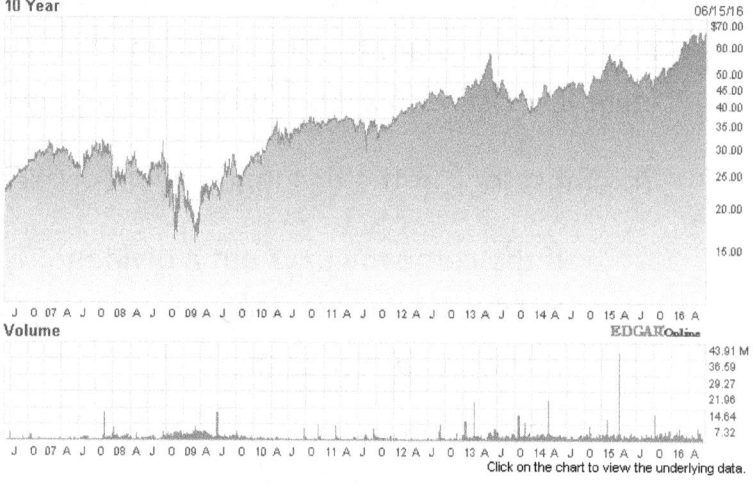

This above example of a 10 year stock chart shows that the stock had a bump in the road in 2007-2009 however it recovered and has had a steady uptrend for 7 years.

Now let's discuss the signs of when a stock is going on a decline and when the stock is going on an upward trend.

Singles that a stock is on the decline is:

Dividend cuts- When the dividend is cut to a lesser amount.

Insider selling- when employees of the company start to sell off their stock in large amounts.

Earnings slow down- when the company's profits start to go on a consistent downtrend.

Industry problems- When an industry goes through a dramatic event, such as oil spills.

Debts are too high- When the company debts are higher than the company's revenue; the company has no way to pay its debts.

Singles that a stock price is about to increase:

Rise in earnings- when there is consistent growth in revenue.

Heavy insider purchasing- when employees of the company start to buy big amounts of the company stocks.

Increase in assets as debts are lower- The Company owns more assets and are no longer strap with debt.

Rumors of takeovers- when a company is acquiring another company to add to their portfolio of assets.

So now we know how to do the research, and we understand what financial statements to look at when we want to make a stock trade. Now let's learn how to make a stock trade.

Chapter 5

How to make a stock trade

Chapter 5

How to make a stock trade

It's actually extremely simple to make a stock trade. It just has a look of complexity. In this chapter I will outline step-by-step on how to do a stock trade. I'm showing this so you can understand the components of your automated trade. In chapter 7 I will show you the steps to do an automated trade. However you must understand the process of doing a regular stock trade first.

The following is an example of an order form that you would use to do a stock trade. Below it is the steps you will follow to complete the trade.

Stock Order Form			
Stock Symbol	WMT	Symbol Lookup	**1**
Transaction	Sell	▾	**2**
Quantity	100	Show Max	**3**
Price	○ Market		
	○ Limit $		**4**
	◉ Stop $ 47.75		
	○ Trailing Stop		
Duration	Good Till Cancelled ▾		**5**
	☐ Send Confirmation Email/Message		
	Preview Order		

Step 1: Fill in the stock ticker/symbol

Step 2: pick if your order type is a buy or sell

Step 3: fill in how many shares (quantity) you are buying

Step 4: fill in what type of stock order you want to use (in this book we focus on market order)

Step 5: Pick the duration of your order, meaning is it a good till cancelled order or day order.

And of course confirm your order once you are done.

I know you're thinking like what, I thought it was harder than that. Unfortunately no, it's just that easy. However we are moving to the hard part, the research.

Chapter 6

Dividends

Chapter 6

Dividends

Dividends over time will be the key to putting you over the top in your investment fund. Compounding dividends and capital gains on your portfolio makes all the difference. So let's take some time out and get to know what a dividend is and the important attributes that we need to know about dividends.

Dividends:

A dividend is a taxable payment declared by a company's directors and paid to shareholders out of the company's earnings. It can be awarded as cash, shares of stock, or company products.

With trading dividend stocks you need to know the following terms:

Ex-dividend- You have to hold your divided stock until the ex-dividend date to receive the dividend. You can sell the stock on ex-dividend date or after and receive the dividend.

Record date- The date established by an issuer of a security for the purpose of determining the owners of the stock, who are entitled to receive a dividend or distribution.

Payment date- The date the company issues dividend payments to all shareholders as of the company set record date.

Date of declaration- This is the date a company reports a quarterly or monthly dividend and the payment date.

Date of execution- The day you initiate the stock transaction (buy or sell).

Closing date- The date on which a stock trade is finalized.

Just a quick note about dividend stocks that you should know:

- A good dividend stock yields 3% or more.
- Good dividend paying industry stock is utilities, real estate, and energy sectors.
- Dividend payout ratio of 50% to 70% is safer.

Investing in dividend stocks you should look at a company's:

1. Steady Income stream

2. Good management

3. Fiscal discipline

4. Earnings transparency

5. Consistent Dividend increase

6. Strong Earnings Growth

7. Strong Revenue Growth

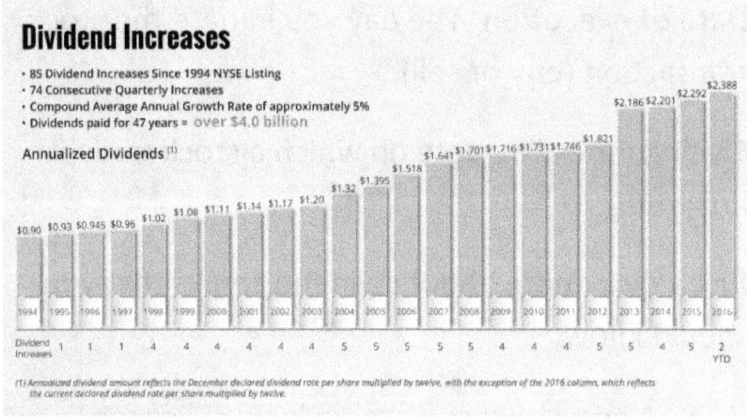

In the above example the growth in dividends easily outperforms any savings account and or certificate of deposit.

Chapter 7

How to automate your investments

Chapter 7

How to automate your investments

Now let's learn how to automate our investment choices. Now there are a lot of places you can go on the internet to make trades. Our goal is to find the most reliable and cheapest in fees to use to trade. I personally use Capital one investing to automate my trades with. With the automated investment strategy especially with capital one investing, you don't have to outright buy the whole share you can buy it bit by bit until you own a whole share. But the object is to do it in a way that you don't have to pay a lot of fees.

For example if you want to purchase a share of Facebook, you can make an automatic plan where every $40 you put into your account goes towards buying a piece of a share. You keep adding $40 in until you get to a total share. But keep in mind you want your fees to be below 8% of your account every month so the bigger the amount you choice to invest with the smaller the fee percentage.

For example if you chose to invest $60 to $100 a month your investment fee percentage would be 8% or less. But if you chose to invest $5 every time your investment fee would be 80% of your investment. Now you can do direct deposits from your checking account to your investment account of $5 a week and once your account hits the total of $60 you can have your account automatically invest into a certain stock you have already picked. It will be a market order trade. You always have the option to sell your stock whenever you choice. The selling of the stock however is not automated you must do that trade on your own. Which is simple, I explained how to do the sell trade in chapter 5.

(DRPs) Dividend Reinvestment Plans

When automating your investments, you should reinvest your dividend payouts into the stock. Regardless of how many shares you own, whatever the dividend payout is can buy a full share to a fraction of a share without being charged a fee to keep investing into the stock. The name of the game is to get fees as low as possible. This form of automated investing is called compounding. This basically means you take the dividends and make them grow along with your shares of stock, by reinvesting your dividend payouts.

Dollar cost averaging (DCA) : which with buying with the automated investing you can buy the stock in regular intervals usually weekly, monthly, bi-weekly over a long period of time. For example if you take $40 a month and invest it in a stock that fluctuates you end up buying less of the investment when it goes up and more of the stock when the price is low. The average price for share is lower than buying a bunch of shares all at once.

To have a dividend reinvestment plan the requirements are to:

1. Be a stockholder for the stock you are trying to reinvest dividends in.

2. You must have a dividend reinvestment option in your account.

3. The stock must pay dividends.

Let's look at the steps to setting up an

automated trade. The following images will help you see the process.

Step one; enter the ticker symbol and the amount you want to invest in that stock. Keep in mind with this trading process you don't have to pay the whole price all at once for the stock; you can buy it in fractions. Also remember to factor in the commission fee; you don't want to pay more than an 8% commission fee. The lessor the fee the better!

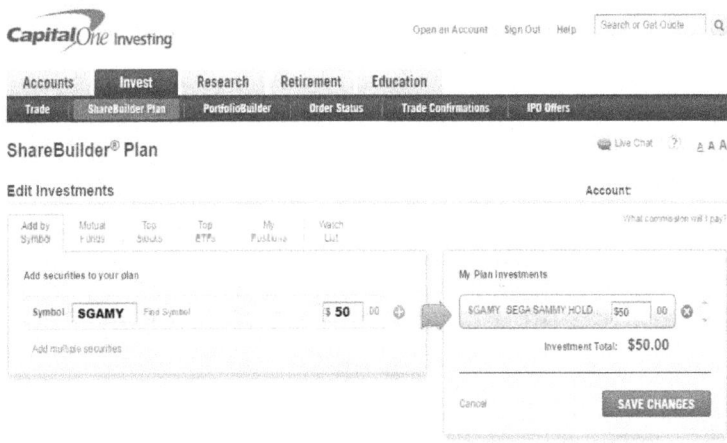

Steps two verify that all the right information is there. Make sure your commission fee is below 8% and click the next button.

With step three you will have to pick from several options how you will fund your account. Once you choose just confirm it and head to the next step.

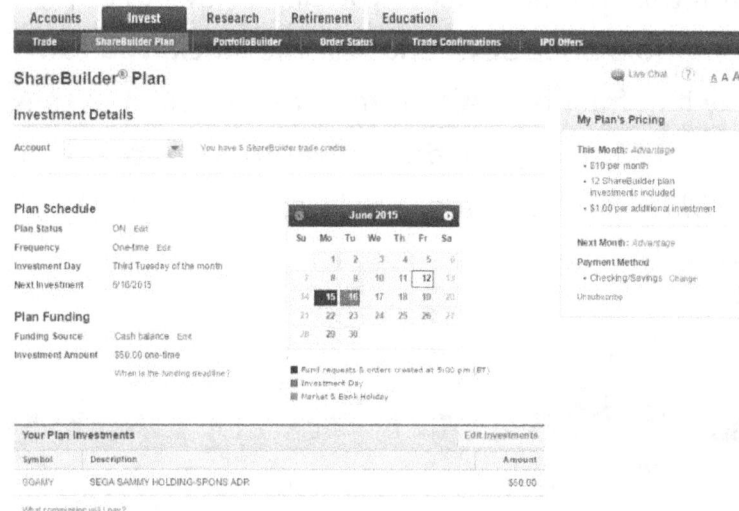

Step four, you look over all your options you have chosen thus far and you confirm your automated plan. Yes it's just that simple!

Chapter 8

Growth plus time plus dividends equals wealth

Chapter 8

Growth plus time plus dividends equals wealth

Now before I close this book out, with gloating about time dividends and capital gains, we need to discuss briefly the tax side of things. As I have said earlier in this book you want to hold your shares of stock for at least a year. Doing this allows you to save on taxes when it pertains to your capital gains and income producing stocks (dividends). See capital gains, is the value of your asset once it increases. The value once the stock increases pass the purchase price. The capital gains tax range from 10% to 39%. You pay this tax once you sell the stock for the profit. Now here's the kicker if you wait that year you will only pay between 10%-15% income taxes. However with capital loss it is not realize till you sell off the stock. Moreover, capital loss is when your asset price is lower than the purchase price of the stock. For the taxes you can use the loss to deduct the taxes on your gains but you can't do it obsessively because that is against the law. Long term capital gain which is stocks held for longer than a year have lower tax rates then short term capital gains. So pay close attention to the timeline that you purchase the stock before you get too excited and try to sell it.

Compounding with the dividend reinvestments and adding time with fractional investments is the key to wealth for any income. Everyone's money can grow no matter the amount. Everybody has the opportunity to use the same wealth tools of time, compounding, and minimum fees. This knowledge has been tested and given now it's up to you the reader, to put it to great use.

Contact info:

Email: woodardholding@gmail.com

Facebook: Woodard holdings

Available now:

Words I never said to my son about running a million dollar business

Available on www.createspace.com/5769927

Words I never said to my son about money and credit

Available on www.createspace.com/5817223

The blueprint to being limitless

Available on

www.createspace.com/5918321

The blueprint to power leadership

Available on

www.createspace.com/5979397

Buy, hold, and sell automated trading for every income

Available now

Coming soon:

Mom I want to be a boss when I grow up

The book I wrote on Facebook

Words I never said to my son about stock trading

Words I never said to my son the gold standard

The blueprint to being limitless

Introduction excerpt

Introduction

When we are born we don't know how to walk, talk, crawl, write, feed ourselves, or even sit up. However our brains are sponges we soak up information and what we see, and eventually we learned all these things. In our younger infant minds we don't hesitate to try to do whatever we want to do, to make ourselves better or to better our intelligence. We don't allow our surrounding as infants to stop us or limit our abilities, so why do we as an adult?

There is no such thing as a limit. Our human brains are limitless. We have the capacity to obtain and hold a lifetime of information. Not just unimportant information, but information that could guide us to an abundant and satisfying life. Unfortunately we limit ourselves, or allow others to limit us because we don't have the strength to overcome and build on those limits thrown at us. We haven't learned how to take those limits, those stones thrown at us and build a foundation from a blueprint lay out to build towards success. We have to be able to structure our minds around the fact that yes every day we will hit a road block or a wall to hold us back or limit us from our full potential but we have to have the courageousness to have already built in us a blueprint to be able to, jump over, climb over, or run through whatever limit is put in our way.

If we build a habit in our own minds that we cannot be stop, and a habit that every day we wake up to this world we run at it with our full potential. Who can deny us? We must build our spirits to be as big as we were born to be. Failure is not an option in life, and for as long as there has been life on this earth failure has not been acceptable or recognized as a positive thing in our society. When we limit our self and our self-worth we set ourselves up for failure.

However we can combat our limits that we encounter on a day to day base. It's truly not hard to make yourself and your life limitless. You just have to put in the work. You can't be scared to open your eyes and mind to new understandings. And you must understand that you need a plan in life to take you to the next level of being limitless.

No matter your situation or your level of education, there is always a way out of problematic situations. The tools that you need to build your blueprint of limitlessness are ambition, determination, focus, the heart to help others, and an open mind. Read and absorb like a sponge to take in knowledge and information. Once you have the tools setup it's time to start developing your blueprint, so let's start building that foundation.

No not all of us can become basketball players, no not all of us can be football stars, but we limit our self when we think that because we didn't become that super star athlete that we can't be the coach that trains an athlete. Or the physical therapist that guides an athlete through the rehabilitation process after an injury. You can still be involved with the sports just in a different way. Don't limit yourself to one side of the playing field know that there are options for every situation.

Life can throw us curve balls that can destroy our will to continue. But it is up to us to see the other side of the situation and not let it hold us back from our true potential. There are no limits to having a full positive limitless life it's all in your thinking. Open your mind to see the other side of all obstacles thrown at you. This book is designed to teach you strategies on how to master turning negativity into positive motivation, how to turn your limits into being limitless and how to build task and to set goals. These are forms that create a limitless form of thinking to change your world.

Stephen Hawking is a theoretical physicist, cosmologist, and author who have Amyotrophic lateral sclerosis (ALS) that has slowly paralyzed him over time. He has been married twice and has three children. He uses a single cheek muscle attached to a speech generating device to communicate. He prepared his lectures in advance with the communication software that he uses to write his speeches. He sends the finish product to a speech synthesizer in sections. When he goes to deliver his speeches, the synthesizer would read it off for the audience to hear. With the same software he used to write his speeches he also authored over 24 books. He showed that no matter your circumstance there is no limit to your ability to live a productive and happy life.

I wrote 70% of my first two books with one hand and in pain with sleepless nights, instead of just watching TV or trolling on social media sites, or sulking in my pain I decided to use my gifts and knowledge and share it with others. So I began to write book after book. I decided to dedicate myself to something other than my physical pain. I say all this to say we complain about the little things in life, when we need to see past the little and see the big picture of not letting the little things box you in. Things could be worse, however only you can be your own limit.

2016